A Trip to Grandma-Mother's House
Chronicles of a Grandma-Mother

Written by
Vanessa Rodgers Tracy

Illustrated by
Whimsical Designs by CJ

Edited by
Shatara S. Clark

Text Copyright © VRT Media, LLC

Illustrations © Whimsical Designs by CJ

Edited by Shatara S. Clark

All rights reserved. No part of this book may be reproduced, transmitted, or stored in an information retrieval system in any form or by any means, graphic, electronic, or mechanical, including photocopying, taping, and recording, without prior written permission from the author.

Printed in the United States of America

ISBN: 9781087990118

DEDICATION

These Chronicles are dedicated to my Grandbabies:

(Mariah, Martell II, Maliah, and Malani)

My time spent with you has added so much joy & laughter to my life. Always remember our fun times together and those teachable moments we shared. Because of you, my world is a brighter place.

You are my LEGACY!

Love,

Grandma-Mother

I have so much fun when my grandbabies come to visit me.

"Hi, Grandma-Mother!"

I am so happy to see them. Every visit is an adventure!

There are plenty of hugs and kisses for everyone.

They love to help water the flowers in my flower garden.

The water helps the flowers grow. Look at the lovely blooms.

We see Mr. Squirrel digging for nuts. He lives in the tree near the flower garden.

Mr. Squirrel always comes out to play when we water the flowers.

"Hello Mr. Squirrel. It's us, Mariah, Martell, Maliah, and Malani," says Mariah.

Mr. Squirrel looks at them, and continues to eat his nuts.

Malani is thirsty!
She tries to drink water
from her pail.

"We did a great job! The flowers are not thirsty anymore Grandma-Mother," says Maliah.

I replied, "Yes! Come stack your pails. I have a surprise for you inside!"

I love baking treats for them.

"Grandma-Mother can I say grace?" Martell asks.

"Yay! We love your cookies Grandma-Mother!"

"Don't forget the milk. Milk makes your bones strong and healthy," I replied.

"Malani loves milk," says Mariah.

"See you next time Grandma-Mother! We will be back to see you soon! Bye, we love you!"

"I love you all too, see you soon! Love you Melody. Drive safely!"

About The Author

Vanessa Rodgers Tracy is a native of Brundidge, Alabama and a Grandma-Mother of four. At an early age she discovered she had a love for writing and reading. Though she loves writing, she especially loves spending time with her Grandbabies Mariah, Martell II, Maliah, and Malani. When she is not with her grandbabies you can find her working in her flower garden. She loves to watch things grow, and she shares this passion with her Grandbabies.

These Chronicles will allow you to be a part of the exciting time spent with her Grandbabies and the adventures they share. Vanessa believes all children should be able to explore their imagination and articulate how they feel. Her first work was published in 1996 in the National Library of Poetry - A Delicate Balance "Whisper In The Wind." Her first novel "Ushered Yet Abandoned, The Mask of A First Lady" was published in 2018.

If you want to learn more about Vanessa's next book, and how you can get a copy, please visit her website at www.vanessartracy.com.

CPSIA information can be obtained
at www.ICGtesting.com
Printed in the USA
BVHW011813301221
625247BV00002B/93